Visualizing Your Victory

WIL CASON

Visualizing Your Victory

VISION PRESS PUBLISHING
Fairfield

Visualizing Your Victory
by Wil Cason

Copyright © 2004 by Wil Cason

Published by Vision Press Publishing
www.visionpresspub.com

ISBN 0-9761325-0-8
Printed in the United States of America

FIRST EDITION

Cover design by Quincy Anderson

Dedication

This book is dedicated to my wife, Kimberly, and our three children: Garrett, Galen, and Kendall. Thank you for inspiring me to inspire others.

The book is also dedicated to my Lord and Savior Jesus Christ for giving me the gift of teaching people throughout the world to visualize victory.

Contents

Acknowledgements

I am truly thankful to the many individuals who have encouraged me on the journey of conceiving and writing this book. First of all, of course, I must thank my wonderful wife and children.

To my editors, Paul Weisser, Ph.D., and Les Wilmont, your feedback and knowledge is truly valuable. Thanks for your patience, dedication, and commitment.

To my mother, Ruthie Anthony, and my four siblings—David, Ellen, Collis, and Shawnee—I appreciate your love and your confidence in my Visualizing Your Victory concept.

To the community members of Bassedena Circle, thank you for modeling a solid moral foundation for my life.

To the members of the Fremont Bible Fellowship, and to Pastor Horacio Jones and his wife, Florence Jones, thank you for your prayers, support, and encouraging words.

Thanks are also owed to my Vision Team: Les Brown, André Chapman, Adrian Davis, John Di Lemme, Peter Ellis, Ph.D., Kevin Lynch, and all the members of Toastmasters Club 4527.

Finally, I am deeply indebted to my graphic designer, Quincy Anderson, and my photographer, Shelia Morgan.

Foreword

The key to achieving your goals and gaining the ultimate success that you've always dreamed of is to have a "vision." Wil Cason has developed a book for champions that will take you step-by-step through creating an empowered vision statement that enables you to "visualize your victory."

By reading this book, taking notes, completing the assignments, highlighting segments, and integrating Wil's techniques into your daily life, you will produce results that will be truly monumental. You will be able to move forward, experience personal breakthroughs, and fully realize your dreams for yourself and your family.

As a motivational speaker and success coach, I would like to thank Wil for acting on his vision and making this book available to a worldwide audience. God bless you, Wil, and your family.

As someone once said, "Without a vision, a man shall perish." Unless you read this book by the great Wil Cason, *your* vision shall perish!

Find Your Why & Fly,
John Di Lemme
August 2004

Preface

There is a large percentage of people who let life lead them—they don't lead their own life. They are satisfied with little more than survival and don't feel they have a chance. They just feel that life is tough and can't get any better. They face life without a vision.

It doesn't have to be that way!

Approaching life without a vision is like driving across the country without a map, which can only result in disappointment and frustration. But vision without application is only an idea. This book will lead you toward your vision and how to accomplish it.

Note to the Reader

Before starting this book, please take a few moments to complete the survey that follows. It will help you to get to know yourself on some important points.

Vision Survey

For each question, circle only one of the numbers.

1 = Very much like me
2 = Somewhat like me
3 = Not at all like me

People of influence are interesting to me.   1 2 3

I have a positive mental image of my personal
and professional future.   1 2 3

I find time to relax and visualize about achieving
positive results.   1 2 3

Setting and reaching goals are critical to my
self-esteem.   1 2 3

I am open to new ideas, and expanding my
knowledge is important to me.   1 2 3

My associate groups are reaching their
professional goals.   1 2 3

I can identify areas of personal stress in my
life and know how to reduce it.   1 2 3

People I interact with are aware of my
leadership skills.   1 2 3

I have a healthy self-image.   1 2 3

I am driven by my thoughts.	1 2 3
I am driven by my emotions.	1 2 3
I am hopeful about my future accomplishments.	1 2 3
I have excellent project-management skills.	1 2 3
I work well with others, and I am reliable.	1 2 3
Procrastination (putting tasks off) is a good way to describe me.	1 2 3
I often find myself motivating and encouraging others.	1 2 3
I am not afraid of healthy challenges.	1 2 3
I know when to make a personal or professional life change.	1 2 3
I can see positive solutions when I am faced with adversity.	1 2 3
I share my goals, visions, and plans with my close associates.	1 2 3
I can identify key individuals to assist me with reaching my visions.	1 2 3
Supporting my company's/employer's vision is important to me.	1 2 3
I am open to receiving constructive feedback.	1 2 3

Scoring the Survey

As you calculate your score, you will discover how helpful this book will be in your life. Scores between 55 and 69 indicate that your life will take a major positive turnaround. Scores between 40 and 54 indicate that you are definitely on the right track, and this book will put you over the top. Scores between 23 and 39 indicate that this book will give you a boost toward maintaining the right path on your journey to success.

A Dream Worth Having Is Worth Living

By March 2003, I was ready. I lit a spark that illuminated the way toward my vision and began to learn the necessary factors for turning a vision into reality. It was clear to me that my passion is writing, speaking, and sharing about vision. I was so excited that for a few weeks it was difficult for me to sleep, so I asked the Lord to direct my steps and use me for His glory. In the middle of the night, I would wake up and write and visualize about doing something different and more meaningful in life.

At the time, I was working in the human services field in northern California. It was going well, and I enjoyed my work. Nevertheless, I knew that there was more for me beyond my traditional job. Furthermore, I wanted to serve more people while I served the Lord. For me, speaking and teaching about vision statements is not a job—it's a calling. (What is your calling?) Believe me, it's gutsy to break out into something new, but I started part-time after work and built up to it. You know, it's really something to have a dream and then live it.

I see, speak about, and seek my vision daily. I share it with people from the cashier at the supermarket to the waiter at the local restaurant. When you start the process of walking in your vision, your life changes and you have a whole new positive attitude. You approach life every day anticipating rewarding experiences. You find that people want to be around you more.

I often tell myself what I see, speak, and seek will produce a harvest. And it's happening! You, too, can speak of hope, excitement, and success in your future.

When Vision Meets Opportunity

One time, in July 2003, my family and I were about to set off on our summer vacation. We were going to visit my mom in Florida for her birthday. The flight from Oakland to Orlando had a brief layover in Nashville. As Kimberly and I got off the plane, we gathered our bags and placed our young sons in their double-stroller.

As we walked through the terminal, we passed a restaurant. We had brought our own sandwiches, but we didn't have any mustard, so Kimberly said, "I'll go check our flight, and why don't you pick up some mustard over there, sweetie."

When I got back with the mustard, she said, "We're going to need a plastic knife to cut the sandwiches."

So back I went for the knife.

"Did you get any napkins?" she asked when I returned.

By now I was slightly irritated, wondering why she hadn't asked for everything in the first place. But I turned around and got the napkins.

Next we had to find a place to sit down and have lunch. Kimberly and I were hungry, and the boys were getting a bit fussy—as one might expect from a two-year-old and a nine-month-old.

As we walked around, looking for a sitting area, I saw someone in the distance who looked familiar.

"No," I thought, "it can't be. Who could I possibly know here? I've never been in Nashville before."

The man was a good three hundred feet away, but I kept my eyes on him, trying to think why he looked so familiar. The closer I got to him, the more convinced I was that I knew him from somewhere.

Then I realized who it was!

I pushed the stroller as fast as I could to catch up to him. The boys were really enjoying the ride!

When I was about fifty feet away, I knew for sure it was him.

I walked up and extended my hand.

"Mister Les Brown," I said, "it's a pleasure to meet you. My name is Wil Cason."

"Where do I know you from, Wil?" he said, shaking my hand.

"Sir, this is our first time meeting. But ten years ago, I saw you on PBS, and you said something I've never forgotten. You said, 'It's better to be prepared for an opportunity and not have one than to have an opportunity and not be prepared.'"

"That's true," he said.

"And since then," I continued, "I've read your books and listened to your tapes, and I'm thankful to be meeting you."

"Wil," he said, "tell me, what do you do?"

"I want to become a motivational speaker," I said.

"Well, as you know," he said, "I train speakers. Give me your business card. And when I call you, don't act like you don't know me."

We both laughed.

After we said goodbye, I was in a daze for the next few minutes. I could literally feel the ground shaking under me.

"Your vision is happening, Wil!" Kimberly said. "You just met your inspiration, Mister Les Brown."

I suddenly realized that if Kimberly hadn't kept sending me back to that restaurant for things, I never would have met Les Brown. That encounter ended up changing the whole course of my life.

Not long after, I was on my way to Atlanta to attend Les Brown's Speakers Network training. That brief, yet powerful, encounter with Mr. Brown, at the airport, had provided me with a path to run toward my vision to become a speaker. Since then, I have spoken on stage with Mr. Brown, hosted my own motivational radio show, and spoken to many national and international audiences.

I believe that whenever vision meets opportunity, there's a groundbreaking experience. Remember, share your vision with everyone around you. Sharing my vision with Mr. Brown propelled me to a new level in the speaking industry, and I'm enjoying every second of it!

Sometimes You'll Feel It's Not Easy

Achieving your vision, whether it's personal or professional, may appear just too difficult. On the path of vision to victory, there will be moments of adversity and setback. Push through, around, under, or over these barriers and focus on your vision statement. That is the light at the end of your tunnel. See yourself already there. That is always the first step!

Take a Chance on Yourself

Back to my dream for a moment. I remember that I wanted to hire a speech coach. I knew that to realize my vision, it was imperative that I invest in my professional development. The coach I wanted to hire, John Di Lemme, was one of the best—a living testament to breaking through life's challenges, since he had developed from a stutterer to a renowned motivational speaker. At that time, John was offering a special rate, but I just didn't have the money. However, with the courage of my vision, I called him and signed up for the program. I figured I'd somehow find a way to pay for it. That was a bold step for me. In the past, I would have said, "Well, I don't have the money, but maybe something will work out next year." In this case, however, an old friend called me a few days later to ask if I were available to work on a project. You know my response!

Now my attitude is that I have the money and need only to determine how to put my hands on it. By changing my mindset to think and see positively, I attracted an unexpected resource. Within a few months, John provided me with exposure and access to an international audience.

Each of us views challenges from a different mindset. Some people see chasms of hopelessness where others see mountains of possibilities. I am truly thankful for developing the confidence and courage to turn my vision into reality. You can experience this same excitement. Just connect your vision to faith, attitude, confidence, and teachability—or what I call FACT. Just ask yourself what you want to achieve and what you are willing to do. The word willing is important here. It sees you through the bumps on the road to getting to your vision.

There will be unforeseen challenges, and some people will even try to discourage you from reaching your vision. Friends asked me, "How are you going to reach your vision? You have a family, full-time job, and do volunteer work." But, remember—others may not see your vision; that's why it's your vision. Don't let anyone prevent you from doing what you know is for you. It turns out that everyone you encounter will benefit from your vision. You have something to give and share with your family, community, and world. Believe it, for it is true. And you know what? We're all in this together!

I understand that some people may feel that the vision process is overwhelming. We all feel that way occasionally. But if you take it in steps, it works. I have found that three key steps will enable you to reach your vision:

1. Clearly state your vision.

2. Build a vision team.

3. Develop a vision action plan.

I have shared these vision steps with family members, friends, and colleagues. After sharing the vision tips, I've seen their attitude, motivation, hope, and ambition change. Currently, they are on a path of achieving their vision, and I anticipate that they will reach tremendous results.

So How Do You Do This?

Look at yourself, your heart, and your purpose. Say it's time to move from vision to victory. Take out a sheet of paper, find a place where you won't be interrupted, and, for at least seven minutes, write down all the reasons that you deserve your vision to come true. Post this list in a place where you will read it daily, such as on the bathroom mirror, the dashboard of your car, or the edge of your computer screen. This is important—constant reinforcement works wonders. See, speak, and believe. Think of a time when you achieved something that you felt good about. What was it? When and where did it take place? How did it happen? Who contributed to it? Capture and reflect on your successful moments and build on them.

This book will provide you with a starting point for visualizing your victory. The key ingredient is you—what you will do after reading this book. When I speak on vision, people will often say to me, "I see where I need to make some adjustments in my life, and I'm looking forward to it." The purpose of this book is to encourage, assist, and challenge you to develop a vision frame of mind and take vision steps. By constructing a vision statement, vision team, and vision plan, you will be doing something that most people never do. A common trait of leaders and high-performing companies is having a vision statement that leads them. They are committed to the vision at all levels of the organization. The vision unifies the organization and directs its efforts to quality work.

Stepping into Your Vision Worksheet

How can you create your vision statement? Here are some key questions to help you:

- Ⲩ How am I preparing myself to move forward toward victory?
- Ⲩ What are some of the hurdles in my life?
- Ⲩ What lessons am I learning that will lead me closer to my vision?
- Ⲩ How will my vision impact the world?
- Ⲩ What must I confess and let go of in order to take a vision step?
- Ⲩ What do I anticipate discovering?
- Ⲩ What can I do every day that will place me closer to my vision?

Start the Process

By reading this book, you are conditioning your mind to move from vision to victory.

See your vision.

Speak of it daily to people around you.

Seek your vision.

Seize your vision.

Moving Forward

I use this process every day to lead me closer to my vision. But sometimes it's difficult to move forward. At those times, I find that it helps to read my vision statement out loud, repeating the process until I am confident again. Knowing that I will overcome any adversity or challenge, I have trust in my vision, understanding that these circumstances are a part of a process to strengthen me. With persistence, I navigate myself to the path, people, place, and performance that will lead me closer to my vision. I have the tenacity to reach victory. And you know what? It really works!

The result of vision is victory. The job loss that my mother, Ruthie Anthony, endured in the early 1980s was a "vision-to-victory" experience for me. She said to me, "Things will get better—just wait and see." I would hear her pray regularly and say, "I believe that joy comes in the morning." She had a positive attitude and encouraged me to see a bright side in her difficult situation.

Within a few months, she had another job. Hopelessness or hopefulness—what you say is what you get. It's up to you. Your words lead your anticipations. See your vision, speak it, and seek it. People who speak words of hopelessness receive what they speak, and, believe it or not, they anticipate it also. You hear them say, "I knew something bad was going to happen—I was waiting for it." The reverse is also true— hopefulness blossoms possibilities.

I remember my mother's words when she said that things would get better. She would recite scripture from the Bible, such as "Faith is the substance of things hoped for, the evidence of things not seen" (Hebrews 11:1).

Your Vision Can Be As Big As You Want

The size of your vision will determine the amount of your return. Are you a person with tremendous vision? Then expect an enormous return!

By reading this book, you are on a journey of building your vision. I encourage you to reach for high performance and productivity.

As you read this book, think about these questions:

- 'Y' What large vision do you want to reach?

- 'Y' What personal life adjustment do you need to address to reach your vision?

- 'Y' When will you commit to taking vision steps?

You will find that you have commitment, confidence, and connections: commitment to reaching your vision daily; confidence that you will reach your vision; and connection with positive people who can provide valuable resources and knowledge to support your vision.

You Want to Get Started—What Do You Do?

The steps are simple. Focus on what is ahead of you, and you will achieve remarkable and unthinkable results.

Step 1

Your vision statement is a written guide to achieve a future result.

- 'Y' State what you want to achieve.

- 'Y' Develop a plan for reaching your vision.

Ϋ Identify and build a relationship with individuals who can help you to reach your vision.

After I delivered a motivational speech one evening on "Visualizing Your Victory," a man approached me and said, "These steps are simple!" He told me that my motivational message changed his life, and he would create his personal vision statement.

Vision is critical to the success of any individual or organization. Think about some friends inviting you on a trip, but not telling you how you would get to your destination. Would you go with them? Then, they tell you that they don't know why they are going. This may sound ridiculous, but I'll bet you know people like that—people who set out on journeys without a map.

A vision statement is crucial. When you develop it effectively, it will provide clear navigation to your destination.

Step 2

Right now, write down something very important that you want to accomplish:

_____

_____

_____

_____

One day, when I was in high school, tryouts were being conducted for the football team. Before trying out, I decided to make a personal T-shirt. I did this to motivate myself to work hard to get on the team. The front of the T-shirt read, "I WILL." The back read, "MAKE THE TEAM." Not only did I make that team, but I was a starter. I wore that T-shirt for the entire season.

Develop a process to push yourself toward your vision. Constantly remind yourself of your future achievement: audiotape it, visualize it, send yourself a voicemail—or even make yourself a personalized T-shirt. Burn your vision statement into your unconscious. You must see, hear, seek, and believe in it in order to be victorious.

Step 3

Visit people where your vision takes place. For example, my vision was to become a world-class speaker and trainer, so I associate myself with other world-class speakers, from whom I can learn. I communicate and network with them.

Decide what you want to achieve and then hang out with people who have already achieved it.

2

Remember Who Your Vision Is For

Your vision is for you and others around you. Your family, community, and the world will benefit from your vision because you will inspire others to move ahead and develop a vision statement.

When you commit to making an investment in yourself, it is a challenging adjustment. When starting the process that I speak of in this book, recognize that:

- Ϋ It's going to be new and will require some adjustments in thinking.
- Ϋ It's imperative that you do it.
- Ϋ It's an investment in yourself.
- Ϋ It's valuable and the payoff is incredible.

Remember, this is a guide that you can add to and customize to fit your own life. I'm sharing with you a few helpful steps that I have observed and practiced. These steps represent a workable process that is open for your ideas, experiences, and knowledge. You know what works best for you. I encourage you to combine your expertise with the steps I am sharing with you.

This chapter will give you the essence of my message. More details and examples of true-life successes fill the remainder of the book. I know you can achieve your vision. Many already have, and many more will.

Developing a Vision

Vision is the ability to see beyond where you are and imagine innovative possibilities. Vision is seeing yourself succeed before you reach success.

Victory is achieving results that add value and strength to your vision. Victory is the end result of visualization.

Have you ever had a vision of accomplishing an exceptional achievement? Remember your excitement when you first critically thought about what was ahead of you? As a speaker and trainer, I work with individuals and teams, assisting them with creating a leading edge vision. Since you are reading this book, you are ready to create your personal vision statement. When a vision is clearly stated and action steps are implemented, powerful accomplishments are reached. Dynamic possibilities are in the mindset of the individual or organization with an emerging vision.

There is a large percentage of people who face life without a vision, which is like dropping a seed on parched ground. This will not produce a harvest. It leads to disappointment, frustration, and hopelessness. Expect your vision to take root and break through the topsoil. Vision without application is only an idea. This book will assist you not only with creating your vision but also with implementing it.

In order for your personal or professional vision to grow into something enormous, the right soil is essential. It works like this:

Sustainability—maintain the momentum.

Observation—watch for growth.

Inclusion—involve others.

Location—choose the right setting or
environment.

Effective leaders all have powerful skills. They can visualize winning possibilities, no matter what the circumstance. These creative thinkers will take one seed or one idea and nurture it into an extraordinary harvest. The soil is your words, thoughts, and actions. I have observed individuals achieving incredible results when they create a positive outlook for their future. They speak with confidence and take the necessary actions to reach their vision. It's amazing to watch people's dreams transform from creative thoughts to blossoming realities.

The ideas in this book on vision have personally and professionally assisted me with reaching excellent results. As I wrote it, I applied the vision steps to my own life. For many years, I thought about working full-time as a speaker and trainer. The instrumental part of this book moved me from thought to action.

Before developing the book, I made several attempts to come out of the starting blocks and pursue a full-time career as a professional speaker and corporate trainer. However, after a few laps, I walked off the track. Three major hurdles obstructed my vision: fear, limited faith, and a lack of focus. To begin with, I spoke self-defeating words. "Wil," I said, "you don't have the money, time, or resources to become a world-class speaker and trainer. You have a good job with benefits, and you're comfortable."

In other words, I was talking myself out of my own future possibilities.

Nevertheless, I knew that my calling was to provide encouragement to others and to share effective strategies to overcome obstacles. I knew many individuals who had a desire to reach for more in life and were looking for practical ways to reach their potential. Several of them told me that they needed help with discovering their vision. I knew that they already contained the answers inside themselves. As Albert Einstein said, "Imagination is more important than knowledge." Feeling my own vision awakening, I passionately desired to help these people find their own visions.

There's a whole new approach when you start the process of walking in your vision. I read and focused on my vision statement every day. When you really commit to your vision, faith, focus, and favor are present all around you.

Moving Closer to Your Vision

Step daily in the direction of your vision. Complete those tasks that lead you at least one step closer to it. Set reachable goals for each day. If the path you are on does not lead to your vision, get off it! Have a magnificent attitude and speak positive words about yourself and your vision. Look for new opportunities and networks that will enrich your vision. Visit places and events where there is potential ground for your vision to grow.

Your Vision Is Calling

The activities in this book can be used in many different settings. I have personally facilitated vision-enriching activities with many individuals, families, teams, and companies. These pages will inspire you to visualize your future accomplishments and take the necessary steps to get outstanding results. People in all sectors of society can benefit from a vision-led mindset. Visionaries lead and guide their teams to reach incredible goals. Are you ready to reach yours?

Achieving Your Vision

Clarifying Your Thoughts

The first phase in achieving your vision is to figure out exactly what you want to achieve and what is preventing you from achieving it.

We all have a burning desire to accomplish something magnificent and meaningful. The ability to think positively about reaching new horizons is fascinating. Imagine that you are a locksmith designing keys to open new doors of opportunity.

Are you excited about moving forward and achieving major results in your life? What things do you need to change in your environment to become more vibrant?

If you were an artist who painted a masterpiece of your own life, what would it look like?

Who are the people around you, and what do they talk about? Which of them support your vision? Your interaction with others is vitally connected with shaping your own ideas of success. High-achieving individuals associate with people who do extraordinary things. How are you creating a positive portrait of your tomorrow?

When you employ the tips from this book, your vision will be enhanced. While gaining this knowledge, you will apply skills to all areas of your life. When you follow the steps described in this book, you will have a more successful professional and personal outlook. After reading this book, you will think about what you want to happen, visualize it, and move on to victory.

Can you see great opportunities and exciting possibilities ahead of you? You will never know how far you can travel until you take the first step. Will you take it now and move toward the direction of your vision? You have it in you to do it. Success awaits.

Have you ever wondered what it is about those few people who consistently attain their resolutions? I believe they have a predetermined vision before they set out on their journey. They have developed a mindset of commitment to completion. People who reach the mark see what it looks like before they get there. With every breath, they experience victory. No matter how difficult the personal or professional challenge, they have a game plan. When implemented correctly, this plan ensures a winning performance. These people like the future better than the past. As Les Brown once said, "Don't go where the path may lead. Go where there's no path, and leave a trail!"

Are you committed to staying on the playing field and not walking away until you have produced a winning performance? Remember, it all starts with you. Today is a new day. What is behind you will not prevent you from reaching your destiny. It's now up to you. What steps will you take to reach your future possibilities? Will you move closer to your vision within the next thirty days?

Begin by keeping a vision journal and recording an account of your progress in it. Title each journal entry "Moving Closer to My Vision."

Pouring a Solid Foundation

Achieving greatness requires building a solid foundation and expecting the absolute best. Would you buy a house that is about to collapse? During the initial phase of looking for a home, people collect information about it. Their purpose is to make a wise decision before making a commitment. The critical component to anything is its foundation, which is similar to a vision statement. The foundation supports the overall structure and holds all the parts in place. Your vision statement is essential to keeping your goals in place and on track. You are in the process of accomplishing your dreams.

There are three concrete elements to pour on your personal or professional foundation: vision, motivation, and purpose.

Vision is the insight and foresight to see beyond where you are today to where you will be tomorrow. Motivation is the inspiration and drive to move forward past all obstacles. Purpose is the reasoning that guides you. Vision, motivation, and purpose are all necessary to develop your personal statement and a winning performance.

While working for large and small sports teams, I have observed athletes at all levels, from amateur to professional. One interesting trait that they all have in common is a vision to achieve victory. Even before a game is played, they all visualize how they will win it. They have a positive attitude and speak of great possibilities. Visionary people wake up daily with a passion to push themselves to a higher level. They have personally committed to do their best, and with each step they seek and find new opportunities. Excitement accompanies most of their conversation. They consistently speak of things they want to accomplish.

Visualize Your Best

What is your vision? Is there something you want to achieve? Your vision may be related to doing well in school, advancing your career, purchasing a new home, increasing your self-esteem, or developing a new product.

Visualization is the ability to see the results before you begin a task. Without that, nothing can ever be accomplished. As Helen Keller said, "the most pathetic person in the world is someone who has sight but no vision."

Visualization is the process of developing confidence that your dream, goal, or plan will come to fruition. You may even have a personal theme, slogan, or proverb to push you to act.

Several sports teams start their off-season with a vision for the following year. Inspiring words help them to focus on future possibilities. Mottoes drive them through the season to anticipate playing in a championship series. They are impelled to perform at their best by visualizing their best.

3

Vision-Led People

People who have a vision and are able to act on it have several characteristics in common:

- ϒ They have a passion to achieve unthinkable results.

- ϒ They place themselves around people, places, and things that will add value to their vision.

- ϒ They motivate others and lead them to reach greatness.

- ϒ They know that patience is vital through any process.

Υ They speak with confidence and purpose.

Υ They grow continuously on both professional and personal levels as part of their vision action plan.

Υ They review their plan and make necessary adjustments when needed.

I have a process that will help you to become one of them.

Creating Your Vision

The attention and dedication you give your vision today will have a direct impact on your future. Go for a solid return on your investment by depositing purpose into your vision account. Withdrawals can only be made after a deposit.

Creating your personal vision breathes life into your future. Try writing down your vision as if you have already accomplished it. For example, Jon always wanted to start his own business in which he would train young people for global employment. In one of my seminars, he wrote the following statement:

> My company, DYNAMIC MINDS®, is a leading edge youth development agency. We have already created international internships for 7,000 high school students.

The key part of this statement is *leading edge youth development agency*, because it tells us exactly where Jon wants to go. It is his guide to success. Every individual needs a vision to reach victory and give them direction.

Now try writing out your own Accomplished Vision Statement.

_____

_____

_____

_____

Jon saw victory in his life. Do you see victory in yours? It is imperative that you look beyond your current situation and see something wonderful. Visualization is seeing beyond where you are.

Here's something I would like you to do. Look at your Accomplished Vision Statement above and reflect on the following questions:

- ϒ How will you feel when you have accomplished your vision?
- ϒ How important to you is reaching this vision?
- ϒ What does your achievement look like?
- ϒ What will you do to attain your vision?

Visualizing your achievement is the major ingredient in building your confidence. But there are other ingredients, including removing the obstacles in your way. For example, who or what is blocking your vision path? When I conduct team-building trainings, I post a large sheet of paper along the wall, which reads:

Imagine how productive this team would be if you move_____ out of your way and make a commitment to _____

_____.

My reason for asking the team members to mentally fill in these blanks is to get them to create a future projection of new possibilities and to make them aware of what is holding them back from success.

I follow up by telling the team that they already have the potential to accomplish their vision. As someone once said, "Continuous effort, not strength or intelligence, is the key to unlocking potential."

Vision Teams

A vision team is a small group of individuals who invest in and add value to your vision. None of us can do the journey alone. Building your vision team is critical. These individuals believe in and support your vision and give you honest feedback. Your team will hold you accountable, reviewing your progress as you develop your vision.

Which people in your life motivate you to set and reach incredible goals? Your vision team members should be loyal individuals who work collectively to help you accomplish your vision. The team should push you to implement each step of your vision. They should not let you fail!

List three people you would consider as primary candidates for your vision team:

1. _____

2. _____

3. _____

What led you to select these individuals? How will they assist you? What do you expect from them? What skills, expertise, knowledge, and resources do they bring to your vision—and will you bring to theirs?

At some time or other, we all require the assistance of others. Individuals have specialties to give and receive. When we share with one another, we increase the probability of reaching our vision. A gathering of people working collectively with a single purpose can produce powerful results.

When creating your vision team, think like a skilled coach, who knows exactly which players are needed to produce winning results. The coach is constantly researching, evaluating, and developing excellent players. Your recruitment plan is to look for individuals who will serve vital roles in your vision.

Creating networks to assist you in reaching your vision is critical to your success. Find people who have visions similar to yours. Ask them what they have experienced on their journey. Their experiences may be different from yours; however, the information you gather from a knowledgeable network can be priceless.

Here are some things to think about at your first vision team meeting:

- 'Y' What things have you already shared with the team about your vision?

- 'Y' What will move you from conversation to demonstration—from saying to doing?

- 'Y' When will you take that first step forward?

Have follow-up meetings to review your progress and to develop a vision plan of action. The action plan will assist you to stay on the path and step toward your vision.

Your team can have as many members as you wish, but probably at least two. When it is assembled, your team will place wings on your vision, and you will soar.

The Vision Action Plan

Now is the time for you to create your vision action plan and commit to it. Your dedication to your vision will help you to push through any adversity, challenges, or difficulties. If you want to succeed, you must give your all.

When I played college football, one of my coaches, Terry Shea, often said to the team, "You must have absolute loyalty to life, education, and sports."

How well *you* perform on game day is a direct result of your accomplishments on practice days. Act as if the game is played *every day*.

Your commitment is the key to opening the door of your vision. No matter how disappointed or rejected you may feel at times, you must continue saying, "I will keep turning the key until the door opens."

Take a few minutes to complete the vision action plan in Table 1 and review it daily.

Table 1: Vision Action Plan

Vision steps I will take	Level of importance	Networking opportunities	Resources I need

I have met many individuals while they were starting their own businesses, developing a new product, going back to school, or enrolling in professional development courses after being laid off from a job. The common theme I heard from these self-starters was, "This is something I always wanted to do, but I never had the time, or I couldn't imagine myself doing it." For years they spent so much time working for a company that they put off their own dreams.

All too often, people have a great idea, but allow it to slip away. What will it take for you to commit to *your* vision? Great ideas are not enough. We all know people who attend conferences, participate in workshops, and read books. They may acquire new knowledge, but they need to develop practical skills to apply it. The first step is to create a plan. This will keep you on course. But how do you apply the vision-to-victory steps on a daily basis?

To begin with, you must apply the steps in *all* areas of your life. For example, when Jon creates his business, he still has to leave quality time for his wife and children. Thus, his vision will permeate every aspect of his life.

Will you move one step closer to your vision by tomorrow? Will your conversation change as you speak of the things you intend to accomplish? Will you go the extra mile to see what opportunities await you? Will you see opposition and adversity as only a process that leads to greatness? Will you continue to step toward your vision and not stop until you have reached it?

Take Action

Some people just talk about their vision. Others just dream about it. But a few turn their vision into victory. What about you? Will you move beyond words to actions? You are filled with power and purpose. Don't let your vision fade away.

No Vision, No Victory

Surround yourself with people who are stepping toward their own vision. You may notice that if your vision is fading, unproductive ideas may creep in. For example, you dwell constantly on the past. Or you feel that the job you have is worthless. Or you decide that you have no interest in learning anything new. This kind of negative thinking only drains your energy and saps your commitment to your goals.

How do you get back on track?

Keep a fresh perspective on your vision. Notice your conversations—are they about the past, present, or future? Evaluate your self-esteem and confidence level. Identify obstacles that are preventing you from reaching your vision. First, we form habits; then they form us. As someone said, "Conquer your bad habits, or they will surely conquer you." Find a purpose for every day, and you will add meaning to your vision. When you close off your ability to dream, you can be devastated. Don't allow your vision to fade.

When telling others about your vision, speak with confidence. Say something like: "I am extremely excited about the remarkable accomplishments that are ahead of me!"

Have a motivational pep talk with yourself—say a few words that drive you to make a positive change of some kind. Make a list of words that motivate you and post them somewhere that you will see them every day. Also, write the words on a small index card and place it in your pocket. Whenever you reach into your pocket, you are reaching into your vision. Allow the card to focus you on your future accomplishments. Go after your dream.

Tables 2 and 3, on the following pages, present positive and negative signs that you may encounter along your path.

Table 2: Signs of Living Visions

▲ Aiming to reach your daily goals
▲ Anticipating great results
▲ Being confident, courageous, and committed
▲ Being willing to take chances
▲ Dedicating time, resources, and talent to your vision
▲ Exciting and inspiring others
▲ Feeling meaningful and worthwhile
▲ Having a positive attitude
▲ Learning continuously
▲ Overcoming adversity
▲ Reaching relentlessly for greater outcomes
▲ Seeing meaningful solutions when faced with difficulties
▲ Seeking innovative opportunities
▲ Sharing your vision with others
▲ Trying new approaches
▲ Weaving your core values into your vision

Table 3: Signs of Dying Visions

- ▼ Acting destructively
- ▼ Avoiding new opportunities
- ▼ Being arrogant or proud
- ▼ Being influenced by negative peer pressures
- ▼ Being reluctant to set new goals
- ▼ Blaming others
- ▼ Developing a poor personal and professional outlook
- ▼ Feeling hopeless
- ▼ Feeling powerless
- ▼ Isolating yourself
- ▼ Lacking confidence
- ▼ Lacking insight into what you want from life
- ▼ Lacking motivation
- ▼ Refusing to invest in personal or professional growth
- ▼ Resisting constructive feedback
- ▼ Talking negatively

In Table 4, make a list of some of your own deteriorating and thriving signs as you pursue your personal and professional vision. Identifying where you are with your vision will help you to make the necessary adjustments to achieve ultimate victory.

Table 4: Signs of My Living and Dying Visions

Signs of a Living Vision	*Signs of a Dying Vision*

Post up Your Vision

When I walk into a company, I immediately look to see if its vision statement is posted anywhere. I also ask the employees what the company's vision is and what contributions they are making to the company's vision. An organization's vision statement describes where the organization wants to be at a certain point in the future. When everyone on a team knows and contributes to the company's vision, the outcome can be tremendous.

The same is true for your individualized vision statement. When people see what you are embarking on, they may want to be a part of it. Are you ready to start stepping toward your vision? Find a place to post your vision statement. Mine is posted in my office right over my desk. I also place positive words and phrases throughout my office to keep me focused on my vision.

See the Vision

Visualization is a healthy skill set. Many top companies recruit individuals who are visionaries. Seeing your vision and believing in your victory will impact your future accomplishments. Your personal vision to victory may relate to academic achievement, career development, personal growth, competence skills, managing stress, or finding a soul mate. Creating a mental picture of what you want will provide you with a winning outlook on success. See yourself becoming a scholar, or starting a new career, or getting married. The key formula that successful individuals use is visualization. They paint a mental picture of success long before they achieve it. Conceptualize your picture of a major accomplishment and take action.

No matter how difficult the process, continue to move forward with commitment and determination to reach your vision. Think about people you know who have accomplished their goals. What did it take for them to do that? I believe they had clear focus, confidence, and a professional network. They were also committed to winning.

I enjoy walking into a sports complex and seeing the home team's motto painted across the wall in bright colors. For example:

"You are entering the land of champions!"

"The road to success starts here!"

"We are committed to winning championships!"

These slogans are visual guides to prepare the team members to think and perform like champions. Before the game is played, the team is already developing a mental and physical capacity to practice like winners.

Commit to self-affirmation by telling yourself that you deserve the absolute best. You can master big things without even realizing it. Your victory is in how you see and approach your task. In challenging situations or in the face of adversity, some people see multiple opportunities where others only see obstacles. What do *you* see when the odds are not in your favor?

Consider the different paths taken by two boys.

There was once an old storyteller named Isaiah, who enjoyed sharing his wisdom with anyone who would listen—which was most folks. One of his stories was about two young boys, Bram and Mack, who were the best of friends and were even born on the same day. On their way to school, they would always talk about what they wanted to do when they grew up. Bram dreamed about becoming a teacher. Mack wanted to become a biomedical researcher.

Bram would share his dream with everyone.

Mack said he was afraid to share his dream with anyone.

Bram pretended to be a teacher every chance he got. He even auditioned for the role of a teacher in the school play.

One day at school was Share Your Dream Day. Bram was totally excited. Mack was nervous.

When Bram spoke before the class, everyone applauded—including the teacher.

When Mack spoke, a few students in the back of the room laughed.

"Sure!" one of them said. "Biomedical researcher! Fat chance you'll ever get *there*!"

After that, even though the teacher reprimanded the heckler, Mack vowed that he would never share his dream again.

The next day, on their walk to school, only Bram talked about his dream.

Mack said, "I'm not sure what I want to do or where I want to go in the future. Everyone laughed at me."

Bram eventually became a very successful teacher, who taught others not only to dream but to *live* their dreams.

Mack, on the other hand, stopped dreaming at all. He allowed the response of others to crush him.

"The point is," said old Isaiah, "it doesn't matter what others say about you. The only thing that matters is what *you* say and believe about yourself."

See Your Victory

Have *you* ever experienced a phase of not knowing what you wanted out of life? You may have felt as if everything around you was falling apart. Athletic coaches will call a timeout and motivate their team when things fall apart. "We can turn this game around," they'll say. "We need every player to be a playmaker. Who will step up and give this game their all?"

The coach first communicates what he or she wants from the team: the desired outcome. Then the coach motivates the team to increase their performance.

Take a personal timeout from your life right now and say what you want. Evaluate your current performance and write out your desired outcome:

I evaluate my performance as_____

_____

_____

My desired outcome is _____

_____

_____

I will stay motivated by _____

_____

_____

Keeping the Vision

To visualize is to be able to see the flip side of any situation. You begin to view challenges as opportunities. You are driven to change discouragement into encouragement.

I remember spending many hours designing a youth support and leadership program for teens. Kimberly created flyers, an online application, and a sophisticated recruiting approach. Then we called potential members, both teenagers and their parents, to invite them to the first meeting. They all said they would come.

On the afternoon of the meeting, right after school let out, Kimberly and I had the room in the community center all set up, and I was ready to give a dynamite motivational speech. Both of us waited nervously for the parents and youth to arrive. The seconds became minutes, and then an hour, and no one walked through that door.

In my mind, I was asking myself what I had done wrong. Should I change this or that, or just walk away and forget about the whole idea? I told myself, "Wait for the vision. It will come—this seed will grow." I started to picture young people coming in the door and enjoying the program. And I also pictured myself working with them enthusiastically and motivating them to do great things. Kimberly also encouraged me to pursue this project, which would be so meaningful, both to the teens and to us.

During the following week, we made more phone calls and passed out flyers. Then, on the day of the next scheduled meeting, Kimberly saw two teenage girls and a boy standing outside the community center. She invited them to attend the leadership program right then and there. They said they weren't sure, but they would take a look at it. However, the session went so well that the teens promised to come back the next week with some friends. Before long, we had ten members.

By visualizing what we wanted, we made it happen.

Vision is the ability to see beyond where you are and imagine innovative possibilities

-Wil Cason

4

I Can Visualize!

Visualizing can produce a harvest of success. Visualize yourself having already achieved your goal. So what have you reached? What does it look like? Feel like? Smell like? Sound like? Taste like? For example, in my vision, I see a sold-out arena with thousands of people listening to my exuberant and powerful message. I can hear them cheering. I can smell cinnamon in the air. I can taste peach cobbler in my mouth. My hands are tingling with excitement. I feel amazed—nervous yet completely confident and grateful.

Key Tips for Visualization

Ψ Find a place where you can be uninterrupted and free to visualize every day.

Ψ In your mind, visit the location of your vision.

Ψ Spend time thinking about being there.

Ψ Use all your senses to materialize your vision.

Ψ Be like a role-playing child, pretending to be a firefighter, teacher, actor, athlete, or scientist.

Ψ Relax and daydream for five minutes.

Ψ Visualize yourself taking action steps.

Ψ Draw a picture of your vision.

Ψ Audiotape or videotape your vision and replay it daily.

Remember, you are the key contributor to walking in your vision. Keep your vision and do not alter it. Trust that your vision will manifest into something magnificent. You must have an attitude of expecting something remarkable, no matter what the circumstances are. When you feel like giving up, don't allow your vision to fade away. Continue to have faith and move forward. Know that your vision has purpose and that people will benefit from it.

Plant your seeds and anticipate groundbreaking experiences. View adversity as a chance for a major breakthrough. In the desert, a visionary will find water. Keep breathing life into your vision, and repeat the words, "My vision shall come." Wake up daily with an expectation to experience something great.

Right now, write down seven positive words that describe your vision:

_____

_____

_____

_____

_____

_____

_____

Vision Portfolio

After you have thought about your vision, start creating a portfolio in which you write about it and place photographs that reflect the vision.

List things below that you would like to photograph:

_____

_____

_____

_____

_____

Words Produce Actions

What you speak is what you will receive. Words can build or break a vision. Have you ever wondered how words influence your actions? Words have a major impact on individuals and the people around them. What words are you depositing into your vision account? What seeds will spring from your words? Will you produce a harvest of success, or will your results be visionless? Your words will define your direction. The words you speak will determine who you become and what you achieve.

Speak words that will lead your vision toward a positive path. Remove self-defeating thoughts, such as "I'm not good enough," or "This is too difficult," or "I'm going to give up." Replace those losing words with winning ones, such as "I'm just the right person to make it happen," or "There's victory waiting for me," or "I'll continue to move forward until I reach my goal."

Remember, what you say is what you get.

Here are a few words to kick-start your thinking process:

> admirable
> awesome
> believable
> brave
> confident
> courageous
> dedicated
> devoted
> empowering
> excellent
> faithful
> fantastic

The following story shows how powerful words can be.

The basketball team at Mission Middle School was down by 22 points. The team captain called a timeout and said to the other players in a loud voice, "We can win this game if we believe we can." Another player said, "They're taller than us and much faster. How can we win?" The captain pointed to a large banner hanging on the wall. In bold letters, it read, "WE ARE THE BEST WHEN WE BELIEVE WE ARE THE BEST." Another player said, "I'm tired of losing. Let's go and take this game." The team returned to the court, turned the game around, and won it. By speaking their vision, they secured a victory.

Change your words and you may change the outcome of your game.

Removing Vision Blocks

Sometimes, people are roadblocks between you and your vision. Their plan is to discourage you from reaching your best. You can become your own vision blocker by talking yourself out of the things you know you can achieve. How do you treat yourself? Some people think that they do not deserve greatness. They even expect the worst of themselves. They go through life complaining about everything. They are so busy being critical that they miss tremendous opportunities.

What is behind you will not prevent you from reaching your destiny. Your past need not be the formula for your future. You are in charge of your future—your past is not in charge!

Make a list of the people who believe in and support your vision:

My Vision Supporters

_____
_____
_____
_____
_____
_____
_____
_____
_____
_____

Now make a list of the people who don't believe in or support your vision.

My Vision Blockers

_____
_____
_____
_____
_____
_____
_____
_____
_____
_____

Plan what you want and share your ideas with at least one of your supporters. Your skills and knowledge will grow while you pursue your vision. Your supporters will add value and encouragement to your life, whereas your blockers will try to deflate your vision.

Once you are aware of the blockers in your life, push them out! If they don't believe in your vision, let them know you are moving on. Do not accept or receive negative comments.

Remember to always see yourself at the peak of your vision before you get there. Act as if you are already there. Wash the negative blockers right out of your hair!

Vision blockers:
- Are intimidated by others' success
- Contaminate others with their negative attitudes
- Demand control
- Feel hopeless and uncertain
- Make critical and negative comments
- Lack confidence in themselves and others

Vision builders, on the other hand:
- Are willing to achieve big dreams
- Encourage leadership at all levels
- Expand their professional knowledge
- Inspire others to set and reach goals
- Reflect on possibilities
- Seek and capitalize on new opportunities

Watching the Garden Grow

During my childhood, I had the fulfilling opportunity to plant several gardens with my maternal grandfather, Enoch Anthony, who took time to teach me the basics of planting.

The first step is to determine what you want to plant and where you want to plant it. Next, you pull out the weeds, clear the ground, and turn the soil. After allowing the ground to sit for two or three days, fertilize and water it. Then plant your seeds. As a child, I was thrilled to see what happened next. Seven to ten days after planting the seeds, I witnessed the miracle of sprouts.

What I learned from planting has been valuable for many life situations. Preparation is vital. When seeds are planted at the right time, in the right place, and with the correct ingredients, they will grow. One pack of seeds can produce a harvest to feed a whole family. Maybe even a whole community.

A vision is like that pack of seeds. One small idea can change your entire life. It's up to you to open your vision pack and plant your seeds.

Have an attitude of expecting a return on your vision. Know and anticipate personal and professional growth. What you see in your life now can be the start of something great.

Growing Vision

I know many individuals who have lived by their visions. Here are the stories of three of them.

Dora launched an outstanding program to start a business and create greater opportunities for teenage girls. Her vision was to link sports and technology in a way that would increase the girls' interpersonal skills. Dora spent long hours developing her program while at the same time taking care of her family and holding down two other jobs. The pursuit of her vision paid off. Within six months, she received an award for developing the best innovative program of its kind. Her vision included developing key networks and expanding professional knowledge. Dora's vision is now meeting the needs of many young women.

Like Dora, Steve had a passion for helping young people. After spending a summer as a volunteer at a children's shelter, he decided that he wanted to start a children's mentoring program. At first, his plan was rejected by several granting agencies, and a few community leaders told him to forget the whole idea. But Steve continued chasing his vision, and eventually he found a sponsor. Beginning modestly with seven staff members, he now has more than 100 employees—all of them working to link elementary school students with mentors.

As a mother of five, Ruthie (who happens to be my mother) raised her children with a biblical foundation and always encouraged them to do their very best. She worked three jobs and was faced with many challenges. But every morning, she prayed for her children and helped them to develop a personal relationship with Jesus Christ. Now, as adults, her children are reaping the benefits of their beloved mother. All of them are leaders in their communities, professions, and churches. Ruthie once said, "We may not have much, but we do have the greatest gifts—love and family."

These exemplary individuals gave all their heart to reaching the full capacity of their vision. No matter what obstacles they had to overcome, they held on to their vision, always believing that there was something greater for them to work toward and achieve. Their vision mattered.

When your vision matters most, you will pursue it relentlessly. As Frank Lloyd Wright once said, "I know the price of success, dedication, hard work, and unremitting devotion to the things you want to see happen."

Proceed with Action

Now that you have the theory, it's time to implement it.

Begin by taking out a sheet of paper and writing down what you most want to achieve. Remember, your pre-vision work involves seeing, speaking, and seeking.

It helps to keep a vision journal and write in it every day to keep a record of your progress. Here are some questions you might address:

'Y' What did you do today that led you closer to your vision?

'Y' How is your vision impacting your life?

'Y' What are you looking forward to achieving tomorrow?

At the end of each week, think about how exciting it will be when you start doing the things you visualized. Take a moment to look back and see your progress. Then think of the possible results in front of you.

Victory

Will you start now to visualize your victory? I have shared with you a few steps to get you started. Combine that with your knowledge and experience to make things happen.

Yes, you can accomplish your vision, because you have what it takes. You can create a vision statement for various aspects of your life: for example, personal, social, spiritual, professional, and financial. Begin the process by filling out Table 5.

Table 5: **Vision Statement**

Write a simple, clear statement of who you are and what you do.

_____

_____

Write two or three power words that describe you.

_____

_____

What are you driven to do or provide?

_____

_____

What is the scale of your vision—local, regional, national, or global?

_____

_____

Who will benefit from your services?

_____

_____

As you work on your vision statement, always remember these points:

- ϒ See yourself there—as if you have already achieved your vision.

- ϒ Every step in the process is valuable and will increase your learning.

- ϒ Your attitude, response, and energy level will indicate who you really are.

- ϒ Have faith.

About the Author

Wil Cason, M.A., is a nationally recognized professional speaker and trainer based in Northern California. He designs and facilitates workshops and seminars on leadership, team building, and interpersonal skills for individuals, groups, and organizations, inspiring them to increase productivity by creating vision statements.

Wil's mission is to encourage people and organizations to reach for more in life to achieve their personal and professional goals. Wil believes that a vision statement is imperative to achieving results. He is currently developing a weekend seminar, "Leading with Vision," that will link personal, team, and organizational vision statements.

photo by Sheila Morgan

Contact Information

As you apply to your life the vision steps described in this book, please consider sharing your results with me by writing to my e-mail address: **wil@wilcason.com**. Also feel free to visit my website: **www.visualizingyourvictory.com**.

When you have developed your vision statement and committed yourself to it, please e-mail me a copy. Your vision statement will make a difference in your life and the lives of the people around you. Take the next step and Visualize Your Victory. I wish you a victorious journey.

If you have additional questions regarding Visualizing Your Victory, please call me toll-free at **(866) 365-7373**.

Thank you!